CLB 2631
© 1991 Colour Library Books Ltd., Godalming, Surrey, England.
All rights reserved
This edition published 1991 by Gallery Books,
an imprint of W.H Smith Publishers, Inc,
112 Madison Avenue, New York 10016
Colour separations by Hong Kong Graphic Arts Ltd., Hong Kong
Printed and bound in Singapore by Tien Wah Press (PTE) Ltd.,
ISBN 0 8317 5989 5

Gallery Books are available for bulk purchase for sales promotions
and premium use. For details write or telephone
the Manager of Special Sales, WH Smith Publishers, Inc,
12 Madison Avenue, New York, New York 10016 (212) 532-6600

Microwave
Fish`n´Seafood

GALLERY BOOKS
An Imprint of W. H. Smith Publishers Inc.
112 Madison Avenue
New York City 10016

Microwave Fish`n´Seafood

A microwave oven is a must if you like fish and seafood. Whether you choose expensive salmon or economical cod, it's perfect cooked in a microwave oven. Fish fillets cook in a few minutes, whole fish take a little longer, but retain their shape and all their delicious flavor and, because microwave cooking preserves all the natural moisture in food, the flesh does not dry out. Shellfish is also ideal for microwaving, as it needs only the briefest cooking.

Our recipe collection of appetizers, soups, main dishes and snacks, introduces you to a whole range of fish and seafoods, both old favorites and more unusual varieties. You"ll find special first courses like Oysters à la Crème and elegant soups such as Smoked Salmon Cream Soup. There is a super-quick recipe for Spicy Potted Shrimps and one for a hearty Cream of Smoked Haddock Soup. Try Poisson Suprême for a lovely dinner party dish, or serve Scampi Provençale in the fastest possible time. If you're doubtful about fish and seafood, these luscious dishes should change your mind.

All microwave recipes were prepared in a 700 watt oven. If your microwave is of a lower output, adjust timings as follows:

500 watt – add 40 seconds for every minute stated in the recipe
600 watt – add 20 seconds for every minute stated in the recipe
650 watt – only a slight increase in the overall time is necessary

OYSTERS À LA CRÈME

SERVES 4

Opening oysters is no trouble when you use your microwave oven to help.

2 dozen oysters on the half shell or unopened
4 tbsps heavy cream
4 tbsps cream cheese
1 tbsp chopped fresh parsley
Salt and pepper
Nutmeg
Coriander leaves to garnish

Step 1 Scrub oyster shells well with a stiff brush.

1. Scrub the oyster shells well, if unopened, and leave to soak in clean water for 2 hours.

2. Arrange in a circle on the microwave turntable and cook on HIGH for 45 seconds to 2 minutes.

3. After 45 seconds insert a short-bladed knife near the hinge and prise open. If the oysters do not open easily, they need further cooking for up to 2 minutes.

4. Remove any pieces of broken shell from the inside and place the oysters in a circle on the turntable.

5. Mix together the heavy cream, cream cheese, parsley and salt and pepper. Top each oyster with some of the cream mixture.

6. Sprinkle with nutmeg and heat through for 2-3 minutes on MEDIUM. Garnish with coriander leaves and serve immediately.

Step 3 Heat for 45 seconds and then open using a short-bladed knife inserted at the hinge.

Step 5 Top each of the oysters with some of the cream mixture.

Cook's Notes

TIME: Preparation takes about 15 minutes, and cooking takes about 5 minutes.

PREPARATION: Add a handful of flour to the soaking water for the oysters. The oysters will expel any sand and take up the flour which will plump them up.

COOK'S TIP: If oyster shells will not sit firmly, place in a microproof dish with ½ inch coarse salt. Press shells into the salt to steady them.

MARINATED SALMON

SERVES 6

_This delicious appetizer of fresh salmon "cooks" in the refrigerator in
its spiced marinade._

½ cup dry white wine
2 tsps white wine vinegar or lemon juice
1 cinnamon stick
1 tsp coarsely ground white peppercorns
1 tbsp crushed coriander seeds
2 whole cloves
1 onion, finely chopped
2 tsps sugar
4 tbsps oil
1lb salmon, filleted and skinned
Curly endive or watercress

1. Combine the white wine, vinegar, spices, onion and sugar in a glass measure.

2. Cook for 6-8 minutes on HIGH. Stir in the oil and allow to cool slightly.

3. Cut the salmon across the grain into thin slices and arrange in a large, shallow dish.

4. Pour over the white wine and spice mixture and leave to cool at room temperature.

5. Cover and put into the refrigerator for at least 4 hours. Serve arranged on a bed of curly endive with a little of the marinade spooned over.

Step 3 Cut the salmon into thin slices across the grain.

Step 4/5 Pour the marinade over the salmon pieces and refrigerate. Turn the pieces in the marinade occasionally.

Cook's Notes

TIME: Preparation takes 20 minutes, although the salmon must marinate for at least 4 hours. The marinade takes 6-8 minutes to cook.

PREPARATION: The salmon pieces are best laid flat to ensure that the marinade "cooks" the salmon evenly.

SERVING IDEAS: If desired, mix 2 tsps Swedish mustard with ⅔ cup mayonnaise and add 2 tsps chopped fresh dill to use as a dressing.

MASALA SHRIMP

SERVES 4

This is a perfect appetizer for an Indian meal. It's spicy, but not spicy hot.

1½lbs large shrimp
2 tbsps oil
1 small onion, finely chopped
2 cloves garlic, crushed
1 tsp ground coriander
1 tsp ground cumin
1 tsp ground mustard
1 tsp ground ginger
1 tsp ground turmeric
¼ tsp ground cinnamon
Pinch cayenne pepper
4 tomatoes, peeled, seeded and diced
2 tsps tomato paste
Juice of ½ lime
Salt and pepper
6 tbsps natural yogurt
2 tsps garam masala
Lime wedges and coriander leaves to garnish

1. Remove the shells from the shrimp but leave on the very tail ends. Wash, devein and pat dry.

2. Put the oil, onion, garlic and spices into a bowl. Cover loosely with plastic wrap and cook on HIGH for 2 minutes.

Step 1 Remove all but the very tail ends of the shrimp shells.

Step 3 Cook the tomatoes until they become soft and pulpy.

3. Mix in the tomatoes, tomato paste, lime juice and seasoning. Cook on HIGH for 3-4 minutes until the tomatoes have pulped.

4. Add the shrimp and cook on HIGH for 3-4 minutes, or until the shrimp are tender and pink.

5. Stir in the yogurt and leave to stand for about 2 minutes before serving.

6. Divide the shrimp between 4 serving dishes and sprinkle each serving with some of the garam masala. Garnish with lime wedges and coriander leaves.

Step 4 Add the shrimp to the dish and cook until pink and tender.

Cook's Notes

TIME: Preparation takes 15 minutes, and cooking takes 11-12 minutes. Allow 2 minutes standing time.

VARIATION: If raw shrimp are not available cook sauce separately and add cooked shrimp during the last minute of cooking time.

SERVING IDEAS: This dish may be prepared in advance and served cold, if desired. Accompany with poppadums.

SALMON AND GREEN PEPPERCORN TERRINE

SERVES 6-8

This elegant fish terrine cooks in only a fraction of the time it would take in a conventional oven.

12 large spinach leaves
1 shallot, finely chopped
12oz plaice or sole fillets, skinned
1lb salmon
1 cup fresh white breadcrumbs
5 tbsps light cream
1 egg white, lightly beaten
Salt
1 cup heavy cream, lightly whipped
1 tbsp green peppercorns

1. Wash the spinach leaves and remove the stalks. Place the leaves in a bowl, cover loosely with plastic wrap and cook on HIGH, in the water that clings to the leaves, for 30 seconds to 1 minute.

2. Rinse with cold water and pat dry with paper towels. Use the leaves to line the base and sides of a terrine or loaf pan, leaving the ends of the leaves overhanging the sides of the dish.

Step 2 Line a glass loaf pan with the cooked spinach leaves.

3. Place the shallot in a small bowl and cover loosely. Cook for 1 minute on HIGH to soften.

4. Cut the plaice or sole fillets into long, thin strips.

5. Skin the salmon and remove any bones. Cut into small pieces. Place in a food processor or blender with the breadcrumbs, light cream, egg white, shallot and salt.

6. Process to a smooth purée. Fold in the heavy cream and green peppercorns by hand.

7. Spread one third of the salmon mixture over the bottom of the terrine dish on top of the spinach leaves. Arrange half of the plaice or sole strips on top and then cover with another third of the salmon mixture.

8. Repeat with the remaining fish strips and salmon mixture. Fold the spinach leaves over the top of the mixture and cover the dish loosely with plastic wrap.

9. Place the terrine in a shallow dish half filled with hot water. Cook on MEDIUM for 14-16 minutes.

Step 7 Layer the fish strips and puréed salmon mixture on top of the spinach.

10. Remove the terrine and leave to cool slightly. Loosen the edges carefully with a knife and invert the terrine onto a serving plate.

Cook's Notes

TIME: Preparation takes 25 minutes. Cooking takes 16-18 minutes.

COOK'S TIP: Rinse the green peppercorns several times in cold water to remove some of their hotness whilst retaining the peppery taste.

SERVING IDEAS: Serve hot with hollandaise sauce or choron sauce from the recipe for Salmon Steaks with Sauce Choron. Serve cold with mayonnaise.

GARLIC SHRIMP AND MUSHROOMS

SERVES 4

Seafood appetizers are always a popular choice and shrimp with mushrooms make an excellent combination.

4-8 oyster or wild mushrooms, depending on size
½ cup butter
1 large clove garlic, chopped
Salt and pepper
Lemon juice
1½ lbs raw shrimp, peeled
2 tbsps chopped parsley

Step 2 Cook the mushrooms in the melted butter with the garlic, seasoning and lemon juice.

1. Leave the mushrooms whole, but remove the stalks. Rinse, if necessary.

2. Melt the butter in a shallow casserole for 30 seconds on HIGH. Add the mushrooms, garlic, salt, pepper and lemon juice. Cook for 2 minutes on HIGH. Remove and set aside.

3. Add the shrimp to the casserole and cook on HIGH for 1 minute, stirring several times.

4. Cook for 30 seconds more on HIGH, if required, to cook the shrimp thoroughly.

5. Mix in the parsley and add more seasoning if necessary. Arrange the mushrooms in individual dishes and spoon over the shrimp and any remaining butter in the dish.

Step 3/4 Cook the shrimp thoroughly.

Step 5 Mix in the parsley and add more seasoning, if necessary.

Cook's Notes

 TIME: Preparation takes about 10 minutes, and cooking takes 3-4 minutes.

 VARIATION: If oyster or wild mushrooms are not available use large flat mushrooms.

 SERVING IDEAS: Accompany with hot French bread.

SPICY POTTED SHRIMP

SERVES 4

This favorite seafood appetizer gets a new flavor with the addition of ground spices to the butter.

12oz cooked fresh or frozen shrimp
¾ cup butter
1 tsp grated nutmeg
½ tsp ground ginger
½ tsp freshly ground pepper
½ tsp paprika
Lemon wedges and small parsley sprigs or dill to garnish

Step 2 Skim any salt from the surface of the melted butter and discard it.

1. If using frozen shrimp, defrost and dry well on paper towels. To clarify the butter, heat on MEDIUM for 2 minutes. Leave the butter to stand for about 15 minutes.

2. Skim the salt from the top of the butter and carefully pour or spoon off the clear butter oil. Discard the milky sediment in the bottom of the dish.

3. Combine the clarified butter and the spices in a clean bowl and cook for 1 minute on HIGH.

4. Stir in the shrimp and spoon the mixture into 6 small custard cups pressing it down firmly.

Step 4 Combine the butter, spices and shrimps and press the mixture into individual custard cups.

5. Spoon over any remaining butter, cover and chill until firm.

6. To serve, turn out the shrimp onto small plates and garnish with lemon wedges and sprigs of parsley or dill.

Cook's Notes

 TIME: Preparation takes about 5 minutes, however, the shrimp will need at least 2 hours to chill until firm. Cooking takes 3 minutes.

PREPARATION: This dish may be prepared a day in advance and kept in the refrigerator.

 SERVING IDEAS: Melba toast or hot whole-wheat toast triangles make good accompaniments.

POTTED SMOKED FISH

SERVES 4

This smooth fish pâté can be prepared well in advance and will keep fresh under a layer of clarified butter.

2 smoked or kippered fish fillets
1 tbsp butter or margarine
1 tbsp all-purpose flour
1/3 cup cream cheese
1/3 cup milk
6-8 pimento-stuffed olives, sliced
2 tsps Dijon mustard
Salt and pepper
1 cup butter for clarifying
Pimento-stuffed olives and black peppercorns to
   garnish

1. Skin the fish fillets and break up into small pieces. Melt butter for 1 minute on HIGH.

2. Stir in the flour and cook for 2 minutes on HIGH. Blend in the cheese, milk, half the olives, mustard and seasoning.

3. Add fish and mix until well blended. Put into four custard cups and smooth the tops of each.

4. Cover individually with plastic wrap and cook for 1 minute on HIGH to set the mixture.

5. Put butter into a medium bowl and heat for 3-4 minutes on HIGH, or until boiling. Leave to stand for 10-15 minutes.

6. Skim the salt off the top and spoon the butter oil carefully over each pot of fish. Fill nearly to the top, and leave until almost set.

7. Place the remaining olives and peppercorns on top of the butter. Chill until set, then cover the decoration with another thin layer of clarified butter and refrigerate again.

Step 2 Make a very thick roux and add the cheese, milk, half the olives, the mustard and seasoning.

Step 3 Stir in the fish and pack the mixture into small dishes.

Step 6 Carefully spoon a layer of clarified butter over the top of each portion.

Cook's Notes

TIME: Preparation takes about 15 minutes, and cooking takes about 8 minutes. The pâté needs at least 2 hours chilling time.

SERVING IDEAS: Serve as a starter or snack with hot ordinary or melba toast or savory biscuits.

COOK'S TIP: Clarified butter can be used to seal pâtés and this will keep them fresh in the refrigerator for several days if the seal is unbroken. It can also be used in conventional cooking for sautéing without the usual danger of burning.

SPARKLING SHRIMP

SERVES 4

Sparkling wine peps up this special occasion appetizer.

Juice and grated rind of half an orange
1 tbsp green peppercorns in brine, rinsed
½ cup sparkling dry white wine
Salt and pepper
1½lbs peeled shrimp
½ cup heavy cream

1. Put orange rind and juice, peppercorns, wine and seasoning into a bowl. Heat for 30 seconds on HIGH.

2. Stir in the shrimp and heat for 1 minute on HIGH.

3. Lightly whip the cream, fold in, and heat for a further 1 minute on HIGH.

4. Adjust seasoning before putting into serving dishes. Garnish with the orange slices.

Step 1 Cook the orange juice and rind with the wine, peppercorns and seasoning.

Step 3 Fold in the lightly whipped cream.

Cook's Notes

 TIME: Preparation takes about 5 minutes and cooking takes 2½ minutes.

SERVING IDEAS: This starter can also be served cold. Allow the wine mixture to cool before folding in the shrimp and cream.

$ BUYING GUIDE: Green peppercorns in brine are available from large supermarkets or delicatessens. Dried and fresh green peppercorns are also available.

BOUILLABAISSE

SERVES 4

This classic fish soup usually takes a lot longer to cook.
The microwave version is just as delicious and so much faster.

12oz assorted fish (e.g. monkfish, red snapper, cod)
8oz assorted cooked shellfish (shrimp, lobster, scallops, crab)
2 leeks, cleaned and thinly sliced
1 small bulb fennel, sliced
1 clove garlic, crushed
2 tbsps olive oil
1 strip orange rind
Few shreds saffron
1 bay leaf
1 tsp lemon juice
3 cups water
½ cup white wine
1 tbsp tomato paste
Salt and pepper
2 tomatoes, skinned, seeded and roughly chopped
1 tbsp chopped parsley
¼ cup prepared mayonnaise mixed with 1 clove garlic, crushed, and a pinch of cayenne pepper
4 slices French bread, toasted

1. Cut fish into 1-inch pieces. Remove shells from shellfish and cut crab and lobster into small pieces.

2. Put the leeks, fennel, garlic and olive oil into a large casserole. Cover and cook for 3 minutes on HIGH.

3. Add the orange rind, saffron, bay leaf, lemon juice, water and wine. Stir in the tomato paste and seasoning and mix well.

4. Add fish and tomatoes and cook for 5 minutes, covered, on HIGH.

5. Add shellfish and parsley, and cook for 2 minutes on HIGH. Leave to stand, covered, for 2 minutes before serving.

6. Mix the mayonnaise, garlic and cayenne pepper and spread on the pieces of toasted French bread. Place the bread in the bottom of the serving dish and spoon over the soup.

Step 1 Cut the fish into even-sized pieces. Remove the crab and the lobster meat from the shells and chop.

Step 6 Place a piece of French bread in the bottom of each serving bowl and spoon over the soup.

Cook's Notes

TIME: Preparation takes about 15 minutes, and cooking takes 10 minutes.

VARIATION: If fresh fennel is unavailable, add 1 tbsp fennel seed.

SERVING IDEAS: If desired, the bread croûtes and garlic mayonnaise may be omitted and the soup served with hot bread.

CREAM OF SMOKED HADDOCK SOUP

SERVES 4

*This soup is rich and wonderfully creamy. It makes a delicious lunch
or light supper with French bread.*

1lb smoked haddock fillets, skinned
2 cups hot fish or vegetable stock
8oz potatoes, peeled and diced
1 large onion, peeled and chopped
2 sticks celery, peeled and diced
Salt and pepper
1 tbsp lemon juice
2 cups milk
2 hard-cooked eggs, chopped
2 tbsps chopped parsley

1. Place the fish in a shallow pan and pour over a few spoonfuls of stock. Loosely cover the dish and cook for 4-5 minutes or until the fish is cooked through.

2. Flake the fish finely, discarding any bones. Set aside.

3. Place the potatoes, onion, celery and remaining stock in a bowl. Cover loosely and cook for about 10 minutes, stirring occasionally during cooking.

Step 3 Cook the potatoes with the onion, celery and stock until fork tender.

4. Add the fish to the potato mixture, season with salt and pepper and stir in the lemon juice. Add the milk.

Step 4 Stir the fish, seasoning and lemon juice into the potato mixture. Do not break up the potatoes too much.

5. Cover loosely and cook for a further 5 minutes on HIGH.

6. Allow the soup to stand for about 2 minutes before serving. Garnish with the chopped hard-cooked egg and parsley.

Step 6 Sprinkle evenly with the chopped egg and parsley.

Cook's Notes

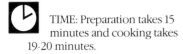 TIME: Preparation takes 15 minutes and cooking takes 19-20 minutes.

 VARIATION: Smoked cod can be used instead of haddock.

 WATCHPOINT: Smoked fish is usually quite salty so season with care.

SMOKED SALMON CREAM SOUP
SERVES 4

This soup is perfect for a dinner party because it tastes so special but is very easy to make.

8oz whitefish, cut into 1-inch chunks
½ cup white wine
3 tbsps butter or margarine
2 tbsps flour
3 cups milk
Pepper
8oz smoked salmon, cut into 1-inch pieces
½ cup light cream
Salt
Sour cream
Chopped chives

frequently, until thickened.

4. Add the pepper, smoked salmon and cream. Blend in a food processor until smooth.

5. Reheat for 1 minute on HIGH loosely covered and add salt to taste. Garnish each serving with a spoonful of sour cream and a sprinkling of chopped chives.

Step 3 Cook the flour, milk, fish and cooking liquid together until thickened.

Step 1 Cook the fish and wine in a loosely covered bowl.

Step 5 Return the puréed soup to the rinsed bowl to reheat.

1. Cook the whitefish and wine for 2 minutes on HIGH.

2. Melt the butter for 30 seconds on HIGH. Stir in the flour, milk, whitefish and its cooking liquid.

3. Cook for 5-6 minutes on HIGH, stirring

Cook's Notes

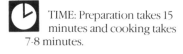 TIME: Preparation takes 15 minutes and cooking takes 7-8 minutes.

 SERVING IDEAS: For special dinner parties add a spoonful of salmon caviar as a garnish.

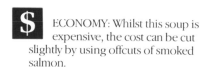 ECONOMY: Whilst this soup is expensive, the cost can be cut slightly by using offcuts of smoked salmon.

WATERZOI

SERVES 4-6

This Dutch fish soup adapts well to microwave cooking. The stock can be made in advance and frozen for later use.

1lb whitefish such as turbot, monkfish, cod or freshwater fish such as pike or perch, skin and bones reserved
Bouquet garni (1 bay leaf, sprig thyme, parsley stalks)
6 black peppercorns
1 tbsp lemon juice
2 shallots, finely chopped
½ cup dry white wine
4oz carrots, cut into thin rounds
2 sticks celery, thinly sliced
2 leeks, well washed and cut into thin rounds
Salt and pepper
Scant 1 cup heavy cream
3 tbsps chopped parsley

carrots, celery and leeks in a large, deep bowl. Cover loosely and cook for about 6 minutes on HIGH, or until the vegetables are nearly tender.

4. Cut the fish into 2-inch pieces and add to the bowl. Season with salt and pepper, re-cover the bowl and cook for a further 6-8 minutes on HIGH or until done.

5. Stir in the heavy cream and leave the soup to stand for 2 minutes before serving.

6. Top each bowl with a sprinkling of chopped parsley before serving. The soup should be thin.

Step 1 Combine the fish bones and trimmings with the water, bouquet garni, black peppercorns and lemon juice to make a fish stock.

Step 3 Cook the vegetables in the stock until nearly tender.

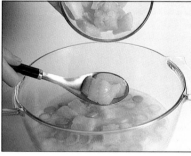

Step 4 Add the fish and cook until all the ingredients are done.

1. Combine the fish bones and trimmings with 1¾ cups water, the bouquet garni, black peppercorns and lemon juice in a large, deep bowl. Cook for 10 minutes on HIGH and then strain.

2. Discard the bouquet garni and the fish bones and trimmings.

3. Combine this fish stock with the shallots, wine,

Cook's Notes

TIME: Preparation takes 20 minutes and cooking takes 12-14 minutes plus 2 minutes standing time.

SERVING IDEAS: Waterzoi is often served with boiled potatoes.

$ BUYING GUIDE: Ready-made bouquets garnis, some especially for fish cooking, are available in the herbs and spices section of supermarkets and delicatessens.

CHEESE AND CLAM CHOWDER
SERVES 4

*Chowders are quick creamy soups that are as filling as a main
course. This one gets its color and flavor from Red Leicester cheese.*

2 tbsps butter or margarine
1 onion, finely chopped
2 sticks celery, chopped
1 green pepper, chopped
2 tbsps flour
½ tsp dry mustard
3½ cups milk
2lbs canned clams, liquid reserved
2 cups potatoes, diced
¼ tsp thyme
Salt and pepper
1 bay leaf
1 cup Red Leicester cheese, grated
Dash Worcestershire sauce
Light cream
2 tbsps chopped parsley

1. Put the butter or margarine, onion, celery and pepper into a large bowl. Cover loosely and cook on HIGH for 2 minutes.

2. Stir in the flour, mustard, milk and clam liquid. Blend well and add potatoes, thyme, salt and pepper.

3. Put in the bay leaf, and cook on HIGH for 10 minutes, stirring occasionally.

4. Remove the bay leaf and add the clams, cheese and Worcestershire sauce. Heat for 2 minutes on MEDIUM to melt the cheese.

5. Add light cream to thin the soup if it is too thick. Garnish with the parsley and serve immediately.

Step 2 Stir the flour and mustard together well before adding the liquid ingredients gradually.

Step 4 Add the clams, cheese and Worcestershire sauce to the soup before heating to melt the cheese.

Cook's Notes

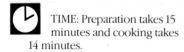 TIME: Preparation takes 15 minutes and cooking takes 14 minutes.

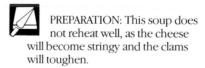 PREPARATION: This soup does not reheat well, as the cheese will become stringy and the clams will toughen.

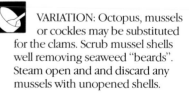 VARIATION: Octopus, mussels or cockles may be substituted for the clams. Scrub mussel shells well removing seaweed "beards". Steam open and and discard any mussels with unopened shells.

CURRIED SHRIMP SOUP

SERVES 4

A quick and colorful soup with the spicy taste of curry and the sharp flavor of apple.

3 tbsps butter or margarine
1 tbsp curry powder
1 shallot, finely chopped
1 apple, peeled, quartered, cored and cut into dice
3 tbsps flour
2 cups fish or vegetable stock
2 cups milk
12oz-1lb cooked, peeled shrimp
½ cup natural yogurt

1. Melt the butter, add the curry powder and cook for 1 minute on HIGH.

Step 2 Stir the shallot and diced apple into the curry powder and butter.

2. Stir in the shallot and apple and cook for a further 2 minutes on HIGH.

3. Stir in the flour and when well blended pour on the stock. Stir well and cook for a further 4 minutes on HIGH, or until thickened.

Step 4 Purée the soup until smooth before adding the milk.

Step 6 Add the yogurt, which can be swirled through the soup using the blade of a knife to make an attractive pattern.

4. Leave to cool. Pour into a food processor or blender and purée until smooth.

5. Add the milk and cook for 1-2 minutes on HIGH.

6. Add the shrimp and leave to stand for 2-3 minutes before serving. Top with natural yogurt.

Cook's Notes

 TIME: Preparation takes 15 minutes and cooking takes 8-9 minutes, plus an extra 2-3 minutes standing time.

 COOK'S TIP: Cooking curry powder or other spices before adding liquid gives them a mellower flavor.

 SERVING IDEAS: If desired, cooked rice may be added to each serving. Heat through before adding the shrimp.

ORANGE BAKED FISH

SERVES 4

*Quick to prepare, this dish uses the tangy taste of orange to offset the
richness of the herring.*

4 herrings
4 bay leaves
4 tbsps butter
Juice and grated zest of ½ orange
1 tbsp chopped dill
Orange slices

Step 1 Place a bay leaf inside each fish, before placing on a sheet of non-stick parchment.

1. Rinse the fish and dry well. Place a bay leaf inside each fish. Place each fish on a sheet of non-stick baking paper.

2. Put the butter in a small bowl and cook on HIGH for 30 seconds to 1 minute to soften slightly.

3. Beat in the orange juice, zest and dill. Divide the butter into four and spread some over each of the fish.

4. Wrap each parcel separately, making sure the fish is totally enclosed.

5. Cook on HIGH for 6-8 minutes, until the fish is cooked, turning the fish parcels halfway through the cooking time. Serve in the paper garnished with orange slices.

Step 3 Spread the orange butter mixture over the outside of each fish.

Step 4 Seal up the parcels of fish twisting the edges of the parchment together.

Cook's Notes

 TIME: Preparation takes 10 minutes and cooking takes 6-8 minutes.

 PREPARATION: If preferred, or if the fish is large, the head and tail of the fish may be removed before or after cooking.

 VARIATION: Other herbs such as tarragon or chives may be used instead of the dill.

 SERVING IDEAS: Green beans and almonds or snow peas make a good accompaniment to this dish.

SIMPLE FISH CURRY

SERVES 4

A delicious curry sauce spices up mild-flavored cod or haddock.

2 tbsps butter or margarine
1 onion, chopped
½ tsp ground turmeric
1 tsp ground cumin
1 tbsp ground coriander
1 tsp paprika
Pinch mace
1 tsp fennel seed
1 tbsp flour
1 cup water
1 bay leaf
1 tbsp chopped parsley
1 tbsp shredded coconut
1lb haddock or cod, cut in large chunks
Chopped coriander leaves

1. Melt the butter in a shallow pan or casserole and add the onion, spices and fennel seed and cook for 2 minutes on HIGH.

Step 1 Cook the fennel seed with the onion and spices in a shallow dish.

2. Add the flour and water and blend well. Add the bay leaf and cook for 5-6 minutes on HIGH to thicken.

Step 2 Add the flour and water and blend together well to make a smooth sauce.

3. Add the parsley, coconut and fish and cook for 3-5 minutes or until the fish is tender.

Step 3 Cook the fish in the sauce until if flakes easily.

4. Remove the bay leaf and garnish with chopped coriander leaves.

Cook's Notes

TIME: Preparation takes about 20 minutes and cooking takes 10-13 minutes.

VARIATION: This dish is also delicious made with shrimp. If using cooked shrimp, prepare sauce and reheat with the shrimp for about 1 minute.

SERVING IDEAS: Serve with plain rice or rice pilaff and a choice of chutney or pickle.

RAIE AU BEURRE NOIR

SERVES 4

Delicious meaty skate cooks so easily in a microwave oven that you can enjoy it in its classic brown butter sauce more often.

4 skinned wings of skate, about 1½lbs in total weight
6 tbsps butter
2 tbsps capers
Juice of 1 lemon
2 tsps chopped parsley
Salt and pepper
Parsley sprigs

Step 1 Arrange the skate wings, thin edges to the center, in a microproof baking dish.

1. Arrange the skate wings in a casserole dish with the thin edges towards the middle. Cover and cook on HIGH for 8-10 minutes.

2. Leave covered while preparing the butter sauce. Heat a browning dish according to the manufacturer's instructions.

3. Add the butter and cook until golden. Add the capers and stir them in the butter for 1 minute.

4. Reheat until the butter is a nut-brown color.

5. Add the lemon juice, parsley, salt and pepper and pour over the fish to serve. Garnish with whole sprigs of parsley if desired.

Step 3 Add the capers to the melted butter in the browning dish.

Step 4 Reheat the butter until nut-brown in color.

Cook's Notes

TIME: Preparation takes 10 minutes and cooking takes 12-14 minutes.

COOK'S TIP: When using a browning dish, always wear oven gloves to handle the hot dish. Also place it on a heatproof mat to protect work surfaces.

VARIATION: Capers are the classic ingredient but, if desired, finely chopped shallot or onion can be substituted and cooked in the butter.

POISSON SUPRÊME

SERVES 4

A classic French dish easily made in your microwave oven — perfect for a fish lovers' dinner party.

4 large plaice fillets, skinned
4 tbsps dry white wine
1 bay leaf
2 parsley stalks
4 black peppercorns
2 tbsps butter or margarine
1 shallot, finely chopped
2 carrots, peeled and cut into thin 2-inch strips
3 sticks celery, cut into thin 2-inch strips
¾ cup mushrooms, sliced
2 tbsps flour
1 cup milk
2 tsps chopped fresh thyme or tarragon
2 tbsps heavy cream
Salt and white pepper

1. Fold the fish fillets in half and place in a shallow dish, thin ends towards the middle. Pour over the white wine and add the bay leaf, parsley stalks and peppercorns.

2. Cover loosely and cook for 5-6 minutes, or until the fish is tender. Pour off and reserve the cooking juices. Leave the fish covered while preparing the sauce.

3. Place the butter in a deep bowl and melt for 30 seconds on HIGH. Stir in the shallot and cook for 2 minutes on HIGH, stirring occasionally until softened.

4. Add the carrots and celery and loosely cover the bowl. Cook for 6 minutes on HIGH, stirring frequently until the carrots and celery are almost tender.

5. Add the mushrooms and stir in the flour carefully. Add the milk gradually, stirring constantly. Re-cover the dish and cook for a further 2 minutes on HIGH, stirring occasionally to keep the sauce smooth.

6. Add the thyme, cream and salt and pepper. Place the fish in a serving dish, cover with the sauce and reheat for 1 minute on HIGH.

Step 1 Fold the fillets in half and place in a round dish with the thickest part to the outside of the dish.

Step 6 Cover the fish with the sauce and reheat in a microproof serving dish.

Cook's Notes

TIME: Preparation takes about 20 minutes and cooking takes 12-13 minutes.

COOK'S TIP: Positioning food so that the thin ends are towards the center of the dish prevents them overcooking.

SERVING IDEAS: Cooked, peeled shrimps makes a good addition to the sauce for dinner parties. Serve the dish with rice or new potatoes.

COD STEAKS WITH MUSHROOMS AND PINK PEPPERCORNS

SERVES 4

A creamy sauce studded with bright pink peppercorns lifts everyday
fish like cod out of the ordinary.

4-8 cod steaks, depending on size
½ cup white wine
1 bay leaf
2 shallots, finely chopped
2 tbsps butter or margarine
1½ cups mushrooms, sliced
2 tbsps flour
½ cup milk
2 tsps pink peppercorns
2 tsps chopped parsley
Grated nutmeg
Salt and pepper

1. Put the cod and wine into a casserole with the thin ends of the steaks pointing towards the middle.

2. Add the bay leaf and shallot. Cover loosely and cook for 6 minutes on HIGH. Leave covered and set aside.

3. Melt the butter in a small bowl for 30 seconds on HIGH. Add the mushrooms, cover loosely and cook for 1 minute on HIGH to soften slightly.

4. Stir in the flour and milk and strain on the cooking liquid from the fish. Add the peppercorns, parsley, a pinch of grated nutmeg and salt and pepper.

5. Cook, uncovered, for 2-3 minutes on HIGH, stirring often until thickened.

6. Remove the skin and bone from the cod steaks if desired and spoon over some of the sauce to serve. Serve the remaining sauce separately.

Step 2 Loosely cover the fish with plastic wrap or with a lid set at a slight angle.

Step 4 Add the peppercorns, parsley, nutmeg and seasoning to the sauce and cook to thicken.

Cook's Notes

 TIME: Preparation takes 15 minutes and cooking takes 9-11 minutes.

 SERVING IDEAS: Serve with rice or new potatoes and a green vegetable such as beans, broccoli or snow peas.

$ BUYING GUIDE: Pink peppercorns, also called pink berries, are available in the spice section of specialist shops and delicatessens.

SALMON STEAKS WITH SAUCE CHORON

SERVES 4

This Hollandaise-type sauce is not difficult to make when you have a microwave oven, and it's delicious with salmon.

4 salmon steaks, about 1½lbs in total weight
½ cup butter
3 egg yolks
Juice and rind of 1 orange
1 tbsp lemon juice
Salt and pepper
2 tbsps heavy cream

1. Pin the ends of the salmon steaks together with wooden picks.

Step 1 Pin the ends of each salmon steak together with wooden picks.

2. Arrange in a round dish with the secured ends towards the middle. Cover loosely and cook on MEDIUM for 8-12 minutes, or until just cooked. Turn the fish over halfway through the cooking time. Leave covered whilst preparing the sauce.

3. In a glass measure, melt the butter for 1 minute on HIGH. Beat the egg yolks with the orange juice and rind, lemon juice and salt and pepper. Stir the mixture gradually into the butter.

Step 3 Gradually add the egg yolk mixture to the hot butter, whisking constantly.

4. Cook on LOW for 15 seconds and whip. Repeat every 15 seconds until the sauce thickens, about 3 minutes. Place the bowl in iced water if the sauce starts to curdle. Stir in the cream.

Step 4 After about 30 seconds, the sauce will begin to thicken. Whisk often to ensure a smooth consistency.

5. Arrange the salmon steaks on a serving dish and pour over some of the sauce. Serve the rest of the sauce separately.

Cook's Notes

 TIME: Preparation takes 15 minutes and cooking takes 11-15 minutes.

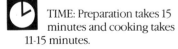 COOK'S TIP: Hollandaise-type sauces are best cooked on a low setting. Medium settings can be used, but watch the sauce carefully. Do not reheat.

 SERVING IDEAS: Serve with asparagus and new potatoes.

WHOLE SALMON

SERVES 6-8

*When you have a microwave oven you can very easily cook a whole
fish with delicious results.*

3½lb salmon, cleaned, with head and tail
    left on
Whole fresh herbs, such as dill or tarragon
Oil for brushing
Lemon slices or wedges
Sliced cucumber
Fresh herbs

---

1. Wash the salmon and pat dry. Place the fresh herbs inside the cavity of the fish and brush the skin on both sides with oil.

2. Use foil to cover the thin end of the tail and the head to prevent overcooking. Wrap the whole fish in several thicknesses of plastic wrap.

3. Make an incision along the skin on either side of the dorsal fin to allow steam to escape and prevent the skin bursting.

4. Lay the fish flat on the turntable, if it will fit, or curve it to fit the shape of the turntable. If curving the fish, tie loosely with string to hold the shape.

5. Cook for 8-9 minutes per 1lb on LOW or DEFROST. About halfway through the cooking time, remove the string and uncover the head and tail to allow them to cook through.

6. To see if the salmon is cooked, slip a sharp knife through one of the slits made on either side of the dorsal fin. If the blade passes through without resistance, the fish is cooked.

7. Allow the fish to cool slightly and then peel away the skin carefully. Start at the dorsal fin with a sharp knife and carry on peeling with a round-bladed table knife which should slip easily between the skin and the flesh.

8. Transfer the fish carefully to a serving plate, removing the herbs from the cavity.

9. Garnish with cucumber, lemon slices or wedges and fresh herbs to serve.

Step 3 Make an incision along the dorsal fin on both sides of the salmon to allow the steam to escape.

Step 4 Tie the head to the tail with a loop of string to keep the fish in a curved shape.

Cook's Notes

 TIME: Preparation takes 20 minutes and cooking takes 8-9 minutes per 1lb of salmon.

 PREPARATION: Skinning fish is much easier whilst it is still warm.

 COOK'S TIP: The foil will deflect the microwaves and the plastic wrap will keep the foil from arcing.

SERVING IDEAS: Serve hot with new potatoes and Hollandaise sauce or cold with mayonnaise and a green salad.

SCAMPI PROVENÇALE
SERVES 4

Sit down to this classic seafood dish in double-quick time with the help of your trusty microwave oven.

2 tbsps olive oil
1 onion, finely chopped
1 clove garlic, crushed
14oz canned plum tomatoes, juice reserved
5 tbsps dry white wine
¼ tsp thyme
1 tsp basil
1 tbsp chopped parsley
1 bay leaf
Salt and pepper
2 tsps cornstarch
1½lbs scampi, shelled

1. Combine the olive oil, onion and garlic in a deep bowl and cook for 5 minutes on HIGH, stirring frequently.

2. Add the tomatoes, wine, herbs, bay leaf, salt and pepper and stir together well. Heat for 2 minutes on HIGH.

Step 2 After adding the tomatoes to the sauce, break them up using a fork or potato masher.

3. Mix the reserved tomato juice with the cornstarch and add to the sauce. Cook for 3 minutes on HIGH and stir well.

Step 3 Stir the cornstarch mixture into the hot sauce to blend smoothly.

4. Add the scampi to the sauce and cook for 2-4 minutes on HIGH or until they are tender and the sauce has thickened. Remove the bay leaf before serving.

Step 4 Cook the scampi in the sauce until they are tender and the sauce has thickened.

Cook's Notes

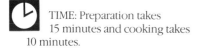 TIME: Preparation takes 15 minutes and cooking takes 10 minutes.

 VARIATION: If scampi are not available, substitute large shrimp.

 SERVING IDEAS: Rice is the usual accompaniment, but why not try pasta for a change?

STUFFED TROUT

SERVES 4

Whole fish cook quickly and evenly in a microwave oven and remain moist and flavorful.

4 tbsps butter
1½ cups fresh white breadcrumbs
2 tsps chopped fresh basil
2 tsps chopped parsley
1 clove garlic, crushed
4oz cooked peeled shrimp, roughly chopped
Salt and pepper
1 egg, beaten
4 trout, cleaned and boned
Juice of 1 lemon
Lemon slices
Whole fresh basil leaves

2. Stir in the breadcrumbs, herbs, garlic, shrimp, salt and pepper and enough egg to bind the mixture together.

3. Sprinkle the insides of the trout lightly with salt and pepper and fill each with some of the stuffing.

4. Place the trout in a large, shallow dish and sprinkle with lemon juice. Cover loosely with plastic wrap and cook for 6 minutes on HIGH.

5. Carefully reposition the trout, re-cover the dish and cook for another 7 minutes on HIGH.

Step 2 Add only enough egg to bind the stuffing ingredients together.

Step 5 Carefully reposition the trout halfway through cooking.

1. Place the butter in a small bowl and heat for 30 seconds on HIGH to melt.

6. Allow to stand for 3 minutes before serving. Garnish with lemon slices and basil leaves.

Cook's Notes

 TIME: Preparation takes 20 minutes and cooking takes 14 minutes.

 COOK'S TIP: Leave the large dorsal fin on each fish. When it pulls out easily, the fish is cooked.

 SERVING IDEAS: This makes an elegant dinner party dish for fish lovers. Serve with new potatoes and asparagus.

PICKLED HERRING

SERVES 4

*Herring in a piquant marinade is a delicious choice for a light lunch.
A microwave oven cooks in all the flavor.*

4 herrings, gutted and boned
1 onion, sliced in rings
½ cup white wine vinegar
½ cup water
4 peppercorns
4 allspice berries
2 tsps mustard seed
1 bay leaf
1 large sprig fresh dill
Salt
1 head lettuce
Fresh dill

glass measure and cook for 6-8 minutes on HIGH.

3. Allow to cool slightly and then pour over the fish. Leave the fish to cool in the liquid, cover and leave in the refrigerator overnight.

4. Serve the fish with some of the onions on a bed of lettuce, and garnish with sprigs of fresh dill if desired.

Step 2 Cook the vinegar mixture until boiling and then allow to cool slightly.

Step 1 Place the herring fillets in a single layer in a shallow dish.

Step 3 Pour the vinegar mixture over the fish, cover and leave to marinate.

1. Separate all the fish into whole fillets removing the heads, tails and fins. Place the fillets in a shallow dish, scatter over the onion and set aside.

2. Mix the vinegar, water, peppercorns, allspice berries, mustard seed, bay leaf, dill and salt in a

Cook's Notes

 TIME: Preparation takes 20 minutes, plus overnight marinating time. Cooking takes 6-8 minutes.

VARIATION: Mackerel fillets may be prepared in the same way.

SERVING IDEAS: Top with sour cream or natural yogurt. Accompany with a salad of fresh beet if desired.

SMOKED HADDOCK WITH PEAS AND PASTA

SERVES 4

This colorful fish and pasta dish tastes as good as it looks. It's ideal for a quick lunch or supper.

8oz smoked haddock fillets
1 cup milk
2 tbsps butter or margarine
2 tbsps flour
3 tbsps frozen peas
1 tbsp chopped chives
1 tbsp chopped parsley
1 hard-cooked egg, chopped
Salt and pepper
8oz pasta shells, cooked

1. Place the smoked haddock in a large, shallow dish and pour over 6 tbsps of the milk, reserving the rest.

2. Cook for 4-5 minutes on HIGH and leave to stand, covered, while preparing the sauce.

3. Melt the butter or margarine for 30 seconds on HIGH in a deep bowl or glass measure.

4. Stir in the flour and pour on the reserved milk. Strain the fish cooking liquid into the bowl and stir well. Cook on HIGH for 3 minutes, stirring once or twice.

5. Add the frozen peas to the sauce along with the chives and parsley. Cook for a further 2-3 minutes on HIGH, or until the sauce is thick and the peas are cooked.

6. Skin and flake the fish, removing any bones. Add to the sauce with the chopped hard-cooked egg and salt and pepper. Stir carefully.

7. Stir in the drained pasta shells. Heat through for 1 minute on HIGH before serving.

Step 7 Combine all the ingredients and return to the microwave to heat through.

 TIME: Preparation takes about 15 minutes and cooking takes 10-12 minutes.

 COOK'S TIP: Pasta can be cooked in a microwave oven. Combine 8oz pasta shapes with 3 cups boiling water. Cook for about 7-10 minutes on HIGH. Cover and let it stand for 5 minutes. Drain and rinse in hot water.

SERVING IDEAS: Serve with a tossed green salad for a light meal.

CRAB AU GRATIN

SERVES 4

Crabmeat in a creamy sauce gives a luxuriously rich flavor to this quick snack.

2 tbsps dry white wine
1 stick celery, finely chopped
1 shallot, finely chopped
7oz jar Cheddar cheese spread
4 tbsps heavy cream, lightly whipped
6oz fresh or frozen crabmeat
4 slices brown bread toast, crusts removed
Paprika
Salt and pepper

Step 3 Add the cream and crabmeat to the softened vegetables and cheese spread.

1. Place the white wine in a deep bowl and add the celery and shallot. Loosely cover the bowl and cook for 2-3 minutes on HIGH, stirring once or twice, until the vegetables are softened.

2. Stir in the Cheddar cheese spread and heat on MEDIUM for 30 seconds or until softened.

3. Stir in the cream and the crabmeat and heat for a further 2 minutes on MEDIUM until piping hot.

4. Arrange the toast in a microproof baking dish and spoon over the cheese and crabmeat mixture.

5. Sprinkle with paprika and heat through on HIGH for 30 seconds to 1 minute. The toasts may be browned under a broiler before serving.

Step 4 Arrange the toast in a circle in a microproof baking dish. Spoon over the crabmeat mixture.

Step 5 Sprinkle the top of the toasts with paprika.

Cook's Notes

TIME: Preparation takes 15 minutes and cooking takes 6-8 minutes.

COOK'S TIP: Cheddar cheese spread can be used any time as a quick cheese sauce. It heats well in a microwave oven without curdling or becoming stringy. Putting the toast on a piece of kitchen paper ensures that the toast stays crisp.

SERVING IDEAS: Serve as a snack or light lunch. Serve with a salad, or put cooked broccoli or asparagus on the toast before topping with the sauce.

SMOKY CHEESE AND SHRIMP DIP

SERVES 4

Delicious as a snack and with drinks, this dip will be a popular addition to your recipe file.

1 tbsp butter
1 shallot, finely chopped
1½ cups Cheddar cheese, shredded
1 cup smoked or smoky cheese, shredded
1 tbsp all-purpose flour
¾ cup light cream
Salt and pepper
¾ cup cooked shrimp, chopped
Raw vegetables

1. Melt the butter in a small, deep bowl for 30 seconds on HIGH.

2. Add the shallot and cook for 1 minute on HIGH to soften.

3. Toss the cheeses and flour together and add to the bowl with the shallot. Stir in the cream, salt and pepper.

4. Cook for 4 minutes on MEDIUM or until the cheese has melted. Stir the mixture twice whilst cooking. Stir in the shrimp.

5. Serve hot with raw vegetables for dipping.

Step 1 Cover the bowl loosely while melting the butter to prevent it spattering.

Step 3 Add the cream to the cheese and butter mixture.

Cook's Notes

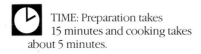 TIME: Preparation takes 15 minutes and cooking takes about 5 minutes.

 PREPARATION: Serve as soon as the dip is made. It does not reheat well.

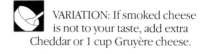 VARIATION: If smoked cheese is not to your taste, add extra Cheddar or 1 cup Gruyère cheese.

SMOKED FISH IN A POTATO

SERVES 4

This recipe only looks complicated. Once prepared and assembled,
these stuffed potatoes are quickly cooked.

4 large baking potatoes
4 small smoked haddock fillets
4 tbsps water
½ cup milk
1 tbsp butter or margarine
1 tsp mild curry powder
2 tbsps butter or margarine
2 tbsps flour
Pinch dry mustard
Pinch cayenne pepper
1 cup milk
½ cup shredded cheese
Salt and pepper
1 tbsp chopped chives
Paprika

1. Wash the potatoes and prick the skins several times with a fork. Bake the potatoes for 10-12 minutes on HIGH.

2. Wrap them in foil and leave to stand for 5 minutes.

3. Place the smoked haddock fillets in a shallow dish with the 4 tbsps water. Cover loosely and cook for 5 minutes on HIGH, or until the fish is tender.

4. Set the fish aside whilst heating the ½ cup milk on HIGH for 5 minutes.

5. Melt the 1 tbsp butter or margarine in a deep bowl for 30 seconds on HIGH. Stir in the curry powder and cook for a further 1 minute on HIGH.

6. Cut a slice off the top of each potato and scoop out the flesh, leaving a border inside the skin.

Step 7 Fill each potato equally with cooked haddock.

7. Skin and flake the smoked haddock, removing any bones. Put an equal portion of fish inside each potato shell.

8. Add the scooped out potato to the curry powder and butter in the bowl and mash well with a fork.

9. Gradually pour in the hot milk and continue mashing until smooth. It may not be necessary to add all the milk, but the potato must be soft yet still hold its shape. Set aside whilst preparing the sauce.

10. Melt the remaining butter or margarine in a small, deep bowl. Stir in the flour, mustard and cayenne pepper.

11. Gradually beat in the 1 cup milk and cook for 3-5 minutes on HIGH, stirring frequently, until thickened. Add the grated cheese, chopped chives and salt and pepper to taste and stir well.

12. Spoon an equal amount of the sauce mixture over the smoked haddock in each potato shell.

13. Pipe or spoon the potato mixture on top and sprinkle with paprika. Cook for 3-4 minutes on HIGH to heat through completely before serving.

Cook's Notes

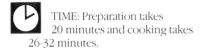 TIME: Preparation takes 20 minutes and cooking takes 26-32 minutes.

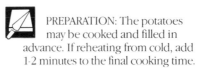 PREPARATION: The potatoes may be cooked and filled in advance. If reheating from cold, add 1-2 minutes to the final cooking time.

 VARIATION: If preferred, the curry powder may be omitted.

SCRAMBLING SHRIMP
SERVES 4

Eggs cook beautifully by microwaves and shrimp added to scrambled eggs make a more interesting dish.

1 tbsp butter or margarine
2 green onions, finely chopped
¼ green pepper, seeded and cut into small dice
¼ red pepper, seeded and cut into small dice
4 eggs, beaten with pepper and salt
½ cup cooked, peeled shrimp

Step 3 Cook the eggs for about 1 minute before stirring for the first time.

1. Melt the butter in a medium-sized bowl on HIGH for 30 seconds. Add the onion and peppers and partially cover the bowl.

2. Cook for 2-3 minutes on HIGH or until slightly softened.

3. Add the eggs to the bowl and cook on HIGH for about 1 minute.

4. Stir well and add the shrimp. Cook for a further 1 minute on HIGH or until the eggs are softly scrambled.

5. Leave to stand for 1 minute before serving. Serve on buttered toast or muffins if desired.

Step 4 Add the shrimp and cook for a further minute, stirring again.

Step 5 Cover and set aside to finish cooking before serving.

Cook's Notes

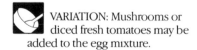

TIME: Preparation takes 15 minutes and cooking takes 4-5 minutes, plus 1 minute standing time.

PREPARATION: During the standing time, the eggs will continue to cook, so don't cook them for too long in the first place. The eggs should be just barely set before standing time.

VARIATION: Mushrooms or diced fresh tomatoes may be added to the egg mixture.

PIZZA MARINARA

SERVES 4

*In only a few minutes you can cook these delicious seafood pizzas to
eat as a snack or as a light meal with a salad.*

4 tbsps tomato paste
1 tbsp dry white wine
1 tbsp water
2 green onions, chopped
½ tsp oregano
1 clove garlic, crushed
¾ cup shrimp, canned or frozen mussels, canned
    or fresh clams or cockles, or a combination of
    all three
8 anchovy fillets
4 black olives, pitted and sliced
2 tsps capers
¾ cup Mozzarella cheese, shredded
2 tbsps Parmesan cheese, shredded
Salt and pepper
4 English muffins, split

1. Mix the tomato paste with the wine, water,
green onion, oregano, garlic, salt and pepper.
Spread the halved muffins with this mixture.

2. Arrange the shellfish on top with a cross of
anchovies. Add the olives and capers and sprinkle
with the Mozzarella cheese.

3. Sprinkle the Parmesan cheese on last and
arrange the pizzas on a paper towel on a plate on
the oven turntable.

4. Cook for 2-4 minutes on HIGH, changing the
position of the pizzas once or twice during
cooking.

5. Leave to stand for 1 minute before serving.
Pizzas may be browned quickly under a preheated
broiler, if desired. Serve hot.

Step 1 Spread the tomato mixture onto the muffin halves.

Step 3 Place topped pizzas on paper towels and arrange on a plate in a circle.

Step 4 Cook on HIGH to melt the cheese and heat the pizzas through. Finish by browning under the broiler, if desired.

Cook's Notes

TIME: Preparation takes about 10 minutes and cooking takes 2-4 minutes plus standing time of 1 minute.

VARIATION: Chopped peppers or sliced mushrooms may be included in the pizza topping.

FREEZING: The pizzas may be prepared in advance and frozen. If freezing, use fresh shellfish or canned tuna fish. Open freeze and wrap individually.

Index

Edited by Jane Adams and Jillian Stewart
Photographed by Peter Barry
Recipes Prepared and Styled for Photography by Bridgeen Deery
and Wendy Devenish
Designed by Claire Leighton, Sally Strugnell and Alison Jewell